SO-AFN-253

GRACE FROM THE CROSS

GRACE FRO

GRACE FROM THE CROSS

KYLE IDLEMAN

BakerBooks

a division of Baker Publishing Group
Grand Rapids, Michigan

© 2018 by Kyle Idleman

Published by Baker Books
a division of Baker Publishing Group
PO Box 6287, Grand Rapids, MI 49516-6287
www.bakerbooks.com

Printed in the United States of America

All rights reserved. No part of this publication may be reproduced, stored in a retrieval system, or transmitted in any form or by any means—for example, electronic, photocopy, recording—without the prior written permission of the publisher. The only exception is brief quotations in printed reviews.

ISBN: 978-0-8010-9364-7

Portions of this text have been adapted from *Grace Is Greater*, published by Baker Books in 2017.

Unless otherwise indicated, Scripture quotations are from the Holy Bible, New International Version®. NIV®. Copyright © 1973, 1978, 1984, 2011 by Biblica, Inc.™ Used by permission of Zondervan. All rights reserved worldwide. www.zondervan.com

Scripture quotations labeled ESV are from The Holy Bible, English Standard Version® (ESV®), copyright © 2001 by Crossway, a publishing ministry of Good News Publishers. Used by permission. All rights reserved. ESV Text Edition: 2011

Scripture quotations labeled Message are from THE MESSAGE. Copyright © by Eugene H. Peterson 1993, 1994, 1995, 1996, 2000, 2001, 2002. Used by permission of NavPress. All rights reserved. Represented by Tyndale House Publishers, Inc.

Scripture quotations labeled NCV are from the New Century Version®. Copyright © 2005 by Thomas Nelson, Inc. Used by permission. All rights reserved.

Scripture quotations labeled NIV 1984 are from the Holy Bible, New International Version®. NIV®. Copyright © 1973, 1978, 1984 by Biblica, Inc.™ Used by permission of Zondervan. All rights reserved worldwide. www.zondervan.com

Scripture quotations labeled NLT are from the *Holy Bible*, New Living Translation, copyright © 1996, 2004, 2015 by Tyndale House Foundation. Used by permission of Tyndale House Publishers, Inc., Carol Stream, Illinois 60188. All rights reserved.

Some of the names and details of people referenced in this book have been changed to protect the privacy of those involved.

Published in association with Don Gates of the literary agency The Gates Group, www.the-gates-group.com.

19 20 21 22 23 24   7 6 5 4 3

In keeping with biblical principles of creation stewardship, Baker Publishing Group advocates the responsible use of our natural resources. As a member of the Green Press Initiative, our company uses recycled paper when possible. The text paper of this book is composed in part of post-consumer waste.

CONTENTS

Introduction   7

1. Who's in the Picture?   11

2. Like the Thief   21

3. Right Where We Are   33

4. New Record   43

5. Jesus Knows   51

6. Scapegoat   61

7. Greater   69

INTRODUCTION

Many of us grew up in church observing the season of Lent leading up to Easter. The tradition of Lent was not established in Scripture. It actually originated in the fourth century as a way to help people prepare their hearts for celebrating the resurrection of Jesus. It's evolved some over the years, but one of the practices of Lent is to give up something during the days approaching Easter. If you grew up observing the season, you may be familiar with this question:

"What are you giving up for Lent?"

What are you going to say no to? What are you going to swear off or let go of? People give up soda, smoking, swearing, watching TV, eating candy, and the list goes on. Let's be honest: for some people Lent is more about going on a diet than getting closer to God. And I've noticed a lot of people give up something for Lent that they won't miss very much. "This year, for Lent, I'm giving up exercise," or "I'm giving up the use of an alarm clock."

Whether you have traditionally observed the season of Lent or not, I want to challenge you to give up something as a way to prepare for Easter. In the days that lead up to Easter, I'm *not* going to ask you to give up movies, or the internet, or Sour Patch Watermelons.

Instead, I want to challenge you to give up something much more personal. Something that maybe you've been holding on to with a white-knuckled grip. As we prepare for Easter, would you be willing to let go of your shame? Would you release the guilt that has been weighing you down? If you are carrying around shame and guilt because of something you've done, would you be willing to give it up for Lent?

I can't think of a more appropriate way to celebrate the greatness of grace this Easter than to receive forgiveness for what you have done and experience God's grace in your life.

To help us let go of these things and fully experience the greatness of God's grace, I invite you to consider some of the last words of Jesus.

It is universally common to attach special significance to the first and last words a person speaks. Parents anxiously await the first understandable syllables their toddler babbles, trying to capture them on video or an audio recording. Similarly, loved ones keeping their bedside vigil during the dying hour of a family member will strain to hear an expressed need or a final request.

The four Gospel writers are consistent in their historical narrative of the event that transpired outside of Jerusalem for six hours on a Friday over twenty centuries ago. By all their accounts Jesus did not say much in his final hours of life on earth. His silence and solitary suffering make the words he does speak that much more impactful.

In the final hours of his earthly time, as Jesus hung on the cross, he made seven statements. These seven sayings do more than reveal the depth of his pain; they declare the greatness of his grace. So let's lean forward and listen carefully to the words Jesus spoke from the cross.

chapter one

Who's in the Picture?

"Father, forgive them."

Luke 23:34

By the time Jesus got to the cross he had been beaten unmercifully.

The Jews had a law for those they flogged—thirty-nine lashes. No more, no less. But Jesus was scourged by the Romans, and the Romans had no such law to govern their scourging. They were experts at beating a man to the edge of his life. (I use the term *experts* loosely, since more than half of those who received this scourging didn't survive.)

Men skilled in torture would whip a condemned prisoner to within an inch of his life. So the skin on Jesus's back, shoulders, and sides was shredded. His face was swollen by the blows from clenched fists and disfigured by the ripping out of his beard by its roots. On his head was pressed a crown of thorns. He was sleep deprived from the night before, as he was led from illegal trial to illegal trial.

So, here's a question: How does someone respond in a situation like this?

The soldiers responsible for carrying out Jesus's execution knew what kind of response to expect. They were used to the drama. They had often heard the agonizing screams, the threats of retaliation, the violent curses. They had seen the thrashing and fighting to try to escape the inevitable torturous death. But Jesus did not react in the ways the soldiers had previously observed. Instead of screaming, threatening, or cursing, Jesus did the unimaginable. He exhaled a short and sincere prayer. "Father, forgive them, for they do not know what they are doing."

He looked out through his own blood, sweat, and tears and extended his grace to "them" in the hour of his death. So, who do you suppose "them" is? Who was he extending his forgiveness to, anyway?

Let's take a census.

He looked out on the *Jewish leaders* who had dogged and opposed him throughout his earthly ministry. For envy they had plotted his death and delivered him up to be crucified, using false witnesses and threats of a riot in the city if the governing authorities did not actively participate in their injustice and violence.

He looked out on the *unfaithful crowd* that had just a week earlier welcomed him into Jerusalem with shouts of "Hosanna in the highest!" but now instead shouted, "Crucify him!" The crowd was likely populated with people who had eaten the loaves and fishes, people who had seen or heard from trustworthy sources the accounts of Jesus's miracle-working power over demons, disease, and death.

He looked out on the *Roman officials and sol-diers*. Pilate rebuffed the counsel of his wife to have nothing to do with Jesus, took the politically expedient route, washed his hands of innocent blood, and delivered Jesus to the crowd for the injustice of a speedy trial and execution. The soldiers were cruel, impersonal, and devoid of compassion for suffering people. Most of them were militant nationalists, hedonists, and materialists. Jesus looked past his bloody feet to see them gambling for his garment at the foot of the cross, and he prayed for God to forgive them.

Jesus also spoke these words over those who were not there that afternoon. He squeezed his eyes closed for a moment and tried to squint through the blood as he looked out into the crowd. All but one of his closest followers had abandoned him. They had run away and disappeared into the night when the mob came to arrest him in the Garden of Gethsemane.

So, for those who had set themselves against Jesus, for those who stubbornly refused to believe that he really is who he says he is, there is grace.

For those who had spoken against him and influenced others to reject him, there is grace.

For those who had followed Jesus for a season but had forsaken him, there is grace.

For those who had chosen to go their own way and live for their own purposes, there is grace.

For those who had consistently pursued their own desires and followed the path of whatever felt good, there is grace.

For those who had timidly gone underground with their faith, scared of what others thought and afraid of being associated with Jesus, there is grace.

But I don't believe Jesus was just thinking about the people who were alive during that time. The Bible says that on the cross Jesus took our sin upon himself. It's not just the Jewish leaders, the Roman soldiers, and the absent disciples to whom Jesus extends forgiveness. In that moment he also made it possible for the offer of forgiveness to be extended to you and me.

▨ ▨ ▨

I read a quote on Twitter the other day from a pastor named Jean Larroux. I inwardly protested as soon as I read it. Ironically, my protest likely did more to prove the truth of what he said. Here's the quote: "If the biggest sinner you know isn't you, then you don't know yourself very well."

My immediate and instinctual response to that quote was, *Well, look, I'm a sinner. In fact, I'm a big sinner. But I'm not the biggest sinner I know.* But the more I think about that quote, and the more I'm honest with myself and my motives, the more difficultly I have denying it.

There was something about that quote that seemed familiar to me. I couldn't quite put my finger on it until I was rereading a familiar passage of Scripture where Paul identified himself as the "chief of sinners." In 1 Timothy 1:15, Paul said to Timothy,

> Here is a trustworthy saying that deserves full acceptance: Christ Jesus came into the world to save sinners—of whom I am the worst.

I remember writing a paper about this passage when I was in seminary. My paper focused on Paul's past before he became a Christian. I made the case that Paul described himself as the worst of sinners because he had been a persecutor of Christians and did everything he could to destroy the church and the cause of Christ. When my professor returned the paper to me, there was no grade at the top of the page. Instead, in red ink, he had written "Rewrite."

I wasn't sure what the problem was. He hadn't made any notes in the margin to help me understand why I needed to start over on the entire paper. I went up to his desk after class, hoping to get a little feedback. He took out his red pen and circled one word from 1 Timothy 1:15.

> Here is a trustworthy saying that deserves full acceptance: Christ Jesus came into the world to save sinners—of whom I **am** the worst.

I waited for a moment, expecting him to expound, but he had already moved on to the next student. I stood there staring at that one word *am*. Suddenly I realized what I had missed. The verb *am* is present tense. And that changed everything. Paul didn't say, "I *was* the worst of sinners." He said, "I *am* the worst of sinners."

If you were to hook me up to a lie detector test and ask me, "Do you think you're the worst sinner?" I would probably say yes because I'm so sinful that I'll try to make myself seem more spiritual by sounding as humble as possible. But I'm fairly certain the polygraph machine would reveal the truth. If I'm honest, deep down—probably not even that deep—I don't consider myself the worst of sinners. But I can tell you, the more I learn about the righteousness of God and the more I examine my own life and motives—the closer I'm getting to the inescapable conclusion that I am the worst sinner I know.

I have discovered a comforting correlation between an awareness of my sin and an appreciation of God's grace. The more honest I have become about the ugliness of my sin, the more humbled I am by the words, "Father, forgive them." There is no getting around the fact that "them" is me.

Do you remember the old hymn that asked the question, "Were you there?" *Were you there when they crucified my Lord? Were you there when they nailed him to a tree?* Take a moment and imagine yourself there. The artist Rembrandt did just that. He painted one of the most famous paintings depicting the crucifixion. At first glance there doesn't seem to be anything out of place. Jesus is hanging on a cross. There's a sign on which they mockingly wrote "King of the Jews." He is surrounded by what appears to be first-century people dressed in first-century clothes. But if you look a little closer, someone there is dressed differently. It is Rembrandt himself. He painted himself into the picture.

Rembrandt paints himself into the scene to make it clear that he is a sinner and it was his sins, along with ours, that sent Jesus to the cross. So, to answer the question of that old hymn—yes, in a very real way you and I were there when ~~they~~ we nailed him to a tree. As we prepare for Easter, don't read these words of Jesus and simply think of the people who were there. Take a moment and paint yourself into the picture.

chapter two

Like the Thief

"Today you will be with me in paradise."

Luke 23:43

As Jesus is dying on the cross, his focus shifts from the masses before him to the man beside him.

We don't know much about this thief. We can only speculate about what his life might have been like before that fateful day. There is no historical data from which we can draw. Even oral tradition doesn't tell us much. We don't know his name or where he was from. We don't know if he had much of a family. Maybe he was a vile criminal who had committed heinous crimes.

Maybe not. Maybe he had just had a run of bad luck. Wrong place, wrong time. We don't know.

We read about this prisoner in the Gospel of Luke, but Matthew also mentions him in passing: "The robbers who were crucified with him also heaped insults on [Jesus]" (Matt. 27:44 NIV 1984). Apparently, both of the men with whom Jesus was crucified mocked and ridiculed him at first. But one changed his mind. Certainly he had heard the talk about this carpenter turned king. Perhaps a cellmate had been in the crowd when Jesus took just fives loaves and two fish and fed thousands. Maybe the blind beggar from whom he had stolen coins was, one day, no longer there by the road. Word on the street was that Jesus had restored his sight. He had likely heard of Jesus before, but now he was seeing Jesus up close in the most desperate and revealing hours of his life.

What he saw and heard changed him from the inside out. He would have been close enough to hear some of the words Jesus spoke from the cross. He probably even heard all seven of the final statements of Jesus.

My guess is that what changed his mind and softened his heart toward Jesus the most was

the prayer Jesus prayed for his accusers and ex-
ecutioners. He didn't pray for their destruction.
I picture ten thousand angels with swords drawn,
waiting for Jesus to say the word. They were ready
to put an end to the injustice and abuse. But he
heard Jesus simply pray, "Father, forgive them."
And this man, the thief, might have wondered
to himself, *Maybe it's not too late for me to be
forgiven.*

Jesus did not pray for the wrath of God to
fall on the resentful Jewish officials, the blood-
thirsty crowd, or the calloused Roman soldiers.
He prayed that God would forgive them. My
guess is something happened in the heart of the
thief when he heard those words, causing him to
do something that Peter failed to do, something
Pilate refused to do, something Jesus's own disciples were afraid to do.

He stood up for Jesus.

In the moment when Jesus felt forsaken, even
by his heavenly Father, a common criminal came
to his defense. Even as the thief on the opposite
cross was hurling insults at Jesus, this criminal
declared, "We are punished justly, for we are getting what our deeds deserve. But this man has

done nothing wrong" (Luke 23:41). What was he saying? He was saying, "I'm wrong—I have sinned—I have fallen short." As his life ebbed away, he was repentant and broken. And he confessed he believed Jesus is the Messiah, the Savior, the promised King. He appealed, "Remember me when you come into your kingdom" (v. 42).

And Jesus said to him, "Truly I tell you, today you will be with me in paradise" (v. 43).

We know less about this thief than any of those who were present at the crucifixion, but we likely have more in common with him than any of the others, because, *like the thief, we have received the promise of salvation but we did absolutely nothing to deserve it.* He could only come to Jesus completely dependent, humble, and broken. He had no other option. But it turns out this is exactly how God wants us to come to him. Like the thief, we must own our sinfulness.

The first three chapters of Romans make it clear we all have sinned. We can deny it. We can defend it. We can justify it. We can rationalize it. We can minimize it. But unless and until we follow this thief's example and accept responsibility for our sin, we can't be saved from it.

The Bible holds up a mirror and confronts us with the reality of our sin. Romans 3:23 teaches:

> Everyone has sinned; we all fall short of God's glorious standard. (NLT)

So, who does "everyone" include? Well, everyone includes you and everyone includes me. We have all sinned. I'm sure you've heard that before. I doubt it's new information. My question is, How do you respond to that information? For a long time, I would read verses like that and think to myself, *Well, yeah. I mean technically, I've sinned. But I haven't sin sinned.* Here's the way it usually gets worded to me: "I'm not that bad."

My wife and I were eating dinner together at a restaurant when a woman, probably in her late fifties, came over and introduced herself. She began to tell her story of how she recently had become a Christian. Except she didn't say "Christian," she said "follower of Jesus." She pointed out her husband seated at a table across the restaurant. I think she felt like she needed to address why he didn't come with her to say hello. She explained he wasn't upset about her decision but seemed annoyed by it and didn't understand. I smiled and waved at him. He waved but didn't smile. His wave was like the wave you give the other driver at a four-way stop when you tell the driver to go ahead even though you think you have the right-of-way. That kind of wave. I went over and introduced myself, and we chatted for a minute or two.

The next day I followed up with an email to both of them saying it had been good to meet them and to let me know if either of them had any questions I could help with. I didn't hear anything back, at least not for a couple of months. And then one day I was sitting at my desk when I got an email from the husband. He told me about the changes he had seen in his wife. She was kinder and more patient. She seemed more joyful. But instead of being excited about these changes, he was skeptical. Here's the line from his email: "She seems much happier now, but I think she's just trying to get me to drink the Kool Aid."

I knew this wasn't a rhetorical email. He was reaching out but didn't want to say it. I emailed him back and asked if he would come to church with his wife and visit with me for a few minutes after a service.

■ ■ ■

We sat in a small room, and I began to tell him the good news of the gospel. I began with Romans 3:23 and made the point that everyone has sinned and fallen short of God's standard. Immediately he became defensive. "I'm not that bad. Most people would consider me a good man." He thought it unfair to be called a sinner and be judged by "God's standard." In his words, "How fair is it to set a standard that no one can meet and then say everyone is a sinner? It's like setting up a target that's out of range and then blaming the shooter for not being able to hit it."

I started my attempt at a theological explanation of why we are sinners. I was going to begin with Adam and Eve in the Garden of Eden and talk about how sin entered the world. I think he would have been impressed with some of the terms I was going to use to explain how we have rebelled against God. But before I had a chance to talk about imputation or ancestral sin, his wife interrupted me and asked if she could say something.

She didn't wait for my permission. She turned toward her husband and said, "Do you think it's ok to get drunk and yell at your spouse? Do you think it's ok to lie about your sales numbers? Do you think it's ok to tell your grandson you'll be at his game and then not show up?" And she asked three or four more personal questions that were clearly indicting. His answers to these questions were obvious. Then she said, "You say it's not fair to be held to God's standard, but you fall short of your own standard."

I had never thought of it that way. We may get defensive when a preacher calls us a sinner—but forget about God's standard; we can't even meet our own standard.

We work hard at convincing ourselves and others we're not that bad, but the truth is we are worse than we have ever imagined. The more we push back on that, the more we push back on experiencing God's grace. If we miss the reality and the depth of our sin, we miss out on the grace of God.

As long as I think I'm not that bad, grace will never seem that good. We usually come to the conclusion we are not that bad a couple of different ways.

1. *We compare ourselves to others.* It's not that we claim to be perfect, but when we compare ourselves to others, what we have done doesn't seem to be that big of a deal. And of course, when we are judging ourselves, we usually give ourselves a big break. Compared to what a lot of people are doing, our sins amount to little more than jaywalking or loitering.

We dismiss our sin and our need for grace by comparing ourselves to others, but do you know what you're doing when you compare yourself to other people and feel superior to them? Yep, you're sinning. And it's likely that from where God sits, your pride and self-righteousness are uglier than the sin of the person you compared yourself to.

2. *We weigh the bad against the good.* Last year, I read a *New York Times* interview with New York City's former mayor Michael Bloomberg. At the time Bloomberg was seventy-two years old. He was being interviewed just before his fiftieth college reunion. Bloomberg talked about how sobering it was to realize how many of his classmates had passed away. But the journalist, Jeremy Peters, observed that Bloomberg didn't seem too

worried about what waited for him on the other side. Peters wrote:

> But if [Bloomberg] senses that he may not have as much time left as he would like, he has little doubt about what would await him at a Judgment Day. Pointing to his work on gun safety, obesity and smoking cessation, he said with a grin: "I am telling you if there is a God, when I get to heaven I'm not stopping to be interviewed. I am heading straight in. I have earned my place in heaven. It's not even close."*

From his perspective, grace wasn't needed or wanted. He put the good he had done on one side of the scale and decided he wasn't going to need any help.

We often find ways to reach the conclusion *I'm not that bad*, but in doing so we miss out on God's great gift of grace. Until we recognize our need for grace, we won't care about receiving it.

* Jeremy W. Peters, "Bloomberg Plans a $50 Million Challenge to the N.R.A.," *New York Times*, April 15, 2014, http://www.nytimes.com/2014/04/16/us/bloomberg-plans-a-50-million-challenge-to-the-nra.html.

Our default is to cover up our sin, or at the very least minimize it. But in covering up our sin, we are covering up grace. In minimizing sin, we are diminishing the joy that comes with forgiveness. Jesus didn't try to make people feel better about themselves by diminishing the seriousness of their sin and falsely reassuring them that they were not that bad.

※ ※ ※

Like the thief, we need to recognize what we deserve for our sin. As Romans 6:23 declares, "The wages of sin is death." It is the punishment we have coming for what we have done and what we have not done. Our sin condemns us to eternal death . . . agonizing permanent separation from the presence of God.

And like the thief, we have been given the undeserved promise of eternal life. Romans 6:23 also says, "The gift of God is eternal life in Christ Jesus our Lord." Jesus promised him, "Today you will be with me in paradise." And in that moment, the worst day of his life became the best day of his life.

I know very little about this thief on the cross and yet I can't help but feel like I know him. We have so much in common. I found myself in a place where I could no longer deny my guilt or pretend that everything was ok. I cried out to Jesus to save me even though I had nothing to offer him in return. He rescued me from the punishment I deserved. One day in heaven I look forward to meeting this thief, finding out his name, giving him a hug, and telling him, "I feel like I know you. What Jesus did for you, he did for me."

chapter three

Right Where We Are

"Woman, behold, your son!"

John 19:26 ESV

We come now to the third saying of grace spoken by Jesus in the hour of his death. The first saying was a prayer of forgiveness for all. The second saying was a promise of salvation for the guilty and condemned. In his third saying from the cross, Jesus offered a word of affection to comfort the brokenhearted. His grace is great enough not just to save us but to sustain us.

Beneath the cross, Jesus saw John standing near his mother. As a mother she was watching her son be tortured to death and was helpless to do anything about it. In that moment, as she was overwhelmed with grief for him, Jesus compassionately passed on the responsibility for Mary's care to John when he said to her, "Woman, here is your son."

As Mary's firstborn, Jesus, according to the custom in that day, would have had the primary responsibility for the provision and welfare of his mother during her advancing years until her death. But Jesus was preceding Mary in death. In recognition of this reality, he officially entrusted his mother's well-being to his disciple John. Jesus knew that she could depend on John in her infirmity and vulnerability. The question might arise, Why was Mary's care not entrusted to one of her other children? It is likely because they had not yet decided to follow Jesus. It was not until after the resurrection that they placed their faith in him. So he knew he could confidently depend on John to provide the spiritual, physical, and emotional care that his mother needed.

■ ■ ■

The Gospels give only brief glimpses of the relationship between Jesus and Mary. But as she stood beneath the cross, seeing her firstborn son in extreme agony, she must have reflected on the day she presented Jesus in the temple.

She would have remembered that moment when old Simeon looked into her eyes and prophesied, "This child is destined to cause the falling and rising of many in Israel . . . so that the thoughts of many hearts will be revealed. And a sword will pierce your own soul too" (Luke 2:34–35). Now was the moment that sword was being cruelly thrust into her. And Jesus suffered because of her suffering. His only tears shed on earth were not for his own suffering but for the suffering of others. He had great grace for the heartbroken, whether their heartbreak was the result of disease, despair, death—or the self-inflicted heartbreak of rebellion, as with the city of Jerusalem's rejection of him.

In some ways this third saying from the cross is the least theological but the most practical. And the practical application of grace is essential. In discussing the gospel of grace, we can sometimes get caught up in the theological aspects, but the greatness of grace is most beautiful when it's up close and personal. The tenderness of grace in this moment is what makes it so great. The concept of grace is attractive from a distance but irresistible when it's personally experienced. The grace Jesus offered Mary reveals the grace available to us in our brokenhearted seasons.

Reading about the grief Mary experienced watching her son die a horrible death on the cross reminds me of one of the first funerals I ever performed. It was for a young man just twenty-five years old. I say "young man," but at that time I was only twenty-one. I had never met him, and the only thing I really knew about him was how he died. It was a drug overdose.

I met with his mother to plan the funeral service. She was a single mom who had just lost her only child. She was a committed Christian but was angry with God and didn't understand why he would let something like this happen. I was fresh out of seminary and had actually written a lengthy paper for my hermeneutics class titled, "Where Is God When Life Is Hard?" I began to address her problem of pain by making my way through some theological talking points. It didn't take long for her to grow tired of my words. Through her tears, anger, and frustration, she said something I'll never forget.

"What does God know about . . ." She didn't finish the sentence. She caught herself. I can't be certain what she was going to ask, but it sounded like she was going to say something along the lines of, "What does God know about *losing a son*?"

Neither of us said anything for a little while. God's grace meets us where we are. God understands the grief Mary felt. Jesus was her son, but Jesus was his son first. God extended his grace to Mary through Jesus as he spoke words of comfort and peace to her.

■ ■ ■

In 2 Corinthians, Paul talks about the sufficiency of God's grace for life's desperate moments. His grace isn't just greater than anything you've done or anything that's been done to you; it's greater than anything you'll ever go through. Paul mentioned what he calls his "thorn in the flesh." We don't know exactly what that was, but it was a circumstance or situation that Paul wanted God to change. In 2 Corinthians 12:9, Paul tells us how God responded whenever Paul asked him to get rid of his thorn: "Each time he said, '*My grace is all you need. My power works best in weakness*'" (NLT, emphasis added). Maybe you memorized that verse as "My grace is sufficient." Another translation says, "My grace is always enough." That's what makes grace so great. There's always enough.

When Peter wrote to Christians who were suffering and facing persecution, he didn't tell them that life would get easier and that everything would get better. He assured them that grace was greater. First Peter 5:12 says, "My purpose in writing is to encourage you and assure you that what you are experiencing is truly part of God's grace for you. Stand firm in this grace" (NLT). No matter what: God's grace is enough.

■ ■ ■

I want you to close your eyes and imagine something. (Ok, that's not going to work, but try to imagine this as you read it.)

In your hand is a simple cup. It's empty, and the emptiness represents your weakness. But someone directs you to a hose nearby. It's coming out of a very high and very long wall. You can't see what's on the other side, but the faucet works. You turn it on and water begins to seep from the hose. It's not spraying—just kind of trickling. You're hoping there's enough to at least fill your cup. It moves right up to the rim, then stops. That worked out well.

You get the symbolism? Right—the water represents God's grace, exactly what we need.

Time passes, and here you come, back to the hose. There's no sign of the cup, but you've got an empty bucket this time. Let's make the bucket a symbol of having a bit of a health scare or maybe some financial issues. You really need some strength; this is a nice-sized bucket.

You turn on the hose and the water comes again, gradually filling in the bottom of the bucket, then up the sides, and once again to the rim before it stops. *How does it know?*

Time passes. This time you are pushing a wheelbarrow. Maybe you've lost your job, and with it your confidence. Or maybe your marriage is in a bad place, worse than you realized. Maybe it's a special needs child and you're overwhelmed. You have a large, red wheelbarrow full of emptiness, and you've brought it to the old hose.

You turn on the hose, and the plumbing still works. The water comes out with that familiar *swish*, and the wheelbarrow begins to fill. And you know where it stops. You sigh with relief. Once again, there's just enough.

Next time you pull up in a semi-truck, hauling a tank behind you the size of a trailer. This is big. Radiation treatments. A child is in prison. An affair. You turn on the hose. Water begins to flow into the truck. You're sure there won't be enough, but it keeps coming. For hours it flows, and then right when the tank won't take another drop, the hose runs dry.

This is how the grace of God works. There is always enough. No matter how much emptiness we bring to him, that is how much grace he has to give us. The emptier we are, the more of his grace we receive.

■ ■ ■

Mary experienced the sufficiency of God's grace in the midst of her incredible grief. In his own greatest hour of need, Jesus was more concerned with his mother's welfare than his own well-being.

In this moment of excruciating physical, spiritual, and emotional pain, Jesus was full of grace and compassion for someone else. His grace to Mary reached out to her right where she was. His grace offered her more than a promise of a far-off happily ever after ending; it cared for her right where she was.

chapter four

New Record

"My God, my God,
why have you forsaken me?"

Matthew 27:46

The fourth saying from the cross is the most anguished of the seven. Jesus "cried out." This is a combination of two ideas: "to shout" and "up." It means "to shout or scream toward heaven."

The messianic Psalm 22 provides us with the most vivid description of Jesus's suffering on Calvary, written centuries before it actually took place. Psalm 22 uses this same word and renders it "roar." It is also the word used of Job's suffering in Job 3. In the agony of his body and soul, Job "cried out" (3:1 NCV) when his food was placed before him. He could not stand to eat and he could not stand not to eat. That's the picture here in Matthew's account. Calvary has been dark and silent for three hours when suddenly Jesus pushes against the nails in his feet and pierces the stillness with an agonizing scream, *"Eli, Eli, lema sabacthani!"* Matthew breaks the Greek narrative with Aramaic, the mother tongue of Jesus, to capture the depth of feeling, the trauma that erupted from Jesus's heart and lips in that moment.

Jesus spoke to his Father three times while on the cross. But only here does he use the more formal name—*Eli* (God). Both of the other times Jesus calls God *Abba* (Dad). *Eli* is indicative of distance and formality, even alienation, and estrangement between God the Father and God the Son. Jesus had never known a time, even before the foundation of the world, when his fellowship with the Father was broken. But now he was experiencing it.

■ ■ ■

On the cross, all the sins of the world were poured out upon Jesus and he "bore [them] in his body on the tree" (1 Pet. 2:24 ESV). God laid on him the iniquity of us all. As a result, the fellowship between God the Father and God the Son was temporarily ruptured. The crushing weight of sin was put on Jesus, and the momentary separation from God is as comparable to the experience of hell itself as you could possibly get. But Jesus was only forsaken temporarily. His Aramaic crying out of a verbatim quote of Psalm 22:1, "My God, my God, why have you forsaken me?" calls to mind the context of this messianic psalm. Perhaps he wasn't questioning the Father, or lamenting the experience of being forsaken by the Father in his most critical hour, as much as he was proclaiming with the psalmist, "Though it may seem like all hope is lost, this is God's finest hour of deliverance!"

Was Jesus questioning the Father, or was he calling to attention that his death on the cross was the fulfillment of Psalm 22? What we do know is that Jesus died our death for sin and he suffered our hell so we would never have to! This is the incredible, incomprehensibly high spiritual cost of grace. Jesus was forsaken so we could be forgiven. At that moment on Calvary, the Bible says that

"God made him who had no sin to be sin for us" (2 Cor. 5:21). Why? That we might become the righteousness of God in him.

■ ■ ■

I have a daughter who is currently applying to attend a number of different universities. When she fills out each application, she is asked to provide "proof of her worthiness." She has to list her grades, her test scores, and any experiences or accomplishments that might make the case she is worthy of being let in, accepted. It's not unlike a résumé for a job or a credit application. The idea is that you are to prove yourself "righteous" enough to be let in. Paul began his letter to the Romans by writing what amounts to a rejection letter to all of us . . . *your application has been denied—your résumé has been rejected.* We are not good enough.

> No one will be declared righteous in God's sight by the works of the law; rather, through the law we become conscious of our sin. (Rom. 3:20)

But there is a righteousness apart from the law, Paul wrote. In other words, a righteousness that is not based on what we have done or what we haven't done . . . it's through faith in Jesus. It's not based on our moral record or our religious résumé. It's a righteousness that comes from God. Look at Romans 3:22–24:

> This righteousness is given through faith in Jesus Christ to all who believe. There is no difference between Jew and Gentile, for all have sinned and fall short of the glory of God, and all are justified freely by his grace through the redemption that came by Christ Jesus.

This is what separates the Christian faith from every other religious system. It's a gift that comes by grace through faith. All the others teach that you have to earn it or pay for it yourself. The Buddhist's eightfold path is based solely on an individual's performance. The Hindu doctrine of *karma* with its successive phases that determine a person's destiny is based on certain things a person accomplished. The good has to outweigh the bad. The Muslims have the code of the law that must be followed precisely in order to enter into paradise. It's all about earning approval and being good enough.

Paul says that righteousness isn't something we earn; it's a gift we are given through Jesus. This is what makes the gospel such Good News—through Jesus we are justified freely. The word *justified* isn't just another way of saying "forgiven" or "pardoned." That's part of it, but it's even better than that. We are not just forgiven of our sin; we are given the righteousness of Jesus, as if it were our own.

■ ■ ■

I've heard the gospel sometimes presented with the word picture of a courtroom. We stand before God, and he pulls out the record of our account, of everything we have done wrong. We start to panic because it's a thick document—thousands of pages. But, as the illustration goes, if we have put our trust in Jesus, those pages are blank. He has forgiven our sins . . . and everything we have ever done wrong has been erased. But God's grace through Jesus is even greater than that. When God pulls out our record, it's not full of our sins and it's not blank. It's actually the perfect and righteous record of Jesus. Your name is on it but it's not your record. It's his record.

The righteousness of Jesus has been transferred onto your record.

The *Message* translation puts it this way:

God put the wrong we did on him who never did anything wrong, so we could be put right with God. (2 Cor. 5:21)

Jesus was *punished* as if he had done everything we have done wrong, and we have been *rewarded* as if we have done everything he has done right.

So, when Jesus was on the cross and cried out, "My God, my God, why have you forsaken me?" it's because our sin record was imputed to him, and it is in that moment that God is making a way for the righteous record of Jesus to be imputed to us. What makes grace so great isn't just that we were deeply in debt and Jesus paid off our debt—it's that we are given the unsearchable riches of Christ.

chapter five

Jesus Knows

"I thirst."

John 19:28 ESV

The fifth saying of Jesus from the cross is a word of suffering. It is the shortest of his seven sayings on the cross. Only two words: "I thirst." We are reminded of the humanity of Jesus in this moment, but most scholars agree these words have a deeper meaning than simply expressing a physical need.

The two most common causes of death in the process of crucifixion were *exhaustion*, because the victim could no longer muster the strength to continually lift himself up, pressing against the nails in his feet and pulling himself up by the nails in his hands to draw another breath, or *dehydration*, because the victim was eventually drained of bodily fluids and parched by the sun and wind. The words of Jesus here speak of the fact that he was experiencing the latter.

Jesus was offered wine three times on the day of his death. The *first time* that he was offered something to drink is recorded both in Matthew and Mark. Matthew records that Jesus was offered a cup of wine mixed with gall, which would have acted as a type of poison. Secretly they might have mixed in ingredients to both hasten death and act as a narcotic to numb his pain. Crucifixion was a long, slow, and agonizing death. This mixture might have relieved Jesus's pain and physical suffering. But Jesus tasted the wine and refused to drink it. He knew the price that had to be paid for our sin and he wasn't looking for a discount.

The *second time* Jesus was offered a drink is around noon. The soldiers were likely not trying to relieve Jesus's thirst as much as to taunt him with the promise of a drink only to withdraw it.

The *third time* he was offered a drink was in response to his words, "I thirst." After his plea, he was offered bitter wine, or sour wine vinegar, but he refused it. So, what do we learn about grace in this two-word declarative from the cross of Christ?

※ ※ ※

This fifth saying, a single word in the Greek language, *reveals Jesus as the promised Messiah*. Jesus stated his thirst not just because he was thirsty but also to fulfill what was written in the Scriptures. In uttering this word on the cross, he fulfilled Old Testament prophecy, revealing his true identity. Of course this was only one of more than three hundred prophecies Jesus fulfilled, a third of which dealt with his death on the cross. Psalm 69:21, in particular, reveals his declaration of thirst. So, this simple saying in fulfillment of Scripture reveals Jesus as the promised Messiah, the Son of God.

This saying shows us Jesus's deity but also reveals his humanity. These two words are words that express pain and physical suffering. We don't often think deeply about his capacity to suffer. But these words give us a window into it. John included this in his Gospel to impress on us Jesus's physical limitations and vulnerability. The incarnation is Jesus confining himself to a corruptible body. Paul wrote,

> [Jesus], being in very nature God,
>> did not consider equality with God
>>> something to be used to his own
>>> advantage;
> rather, he made himself nothing
>> by taking the very nature of a servant,
>> being made in human likeness.
> And being found in appearance as a
> man,
>> he humbled himself
>> by becoming obedient to death—
>>> even death on a cross! (Phil.
>>> 2:6–8)

The humanity of Jesus expressed in his simple declaration of thirst reminds us of a powerful truth: *Jesus knows what it's like.* Before coming to this earth, Jesus might have known about our struggles. He was cognitively aware of human pain and suffering. But there is a big difference between *knowing about* suffering and *knowing* suffering. I often see this when I visit some of our support groups at church. If I visit a grief recovery group, a single mom's group, or an AA or an NA group, I can do my best to offer support and encouragement, and they might appreciate it, but I imagine in the back of their minds they are thinking, *That's nice and all, but he doesn't know what it's like.* There is a certain comfort in simply knowing that Jesus knows. He knows what it's like.

■ ■ ■

I was recently having breakfast with a father who shared with me some of the challenges of having a child with special needs. He knew he and his wife needed help and support, but he wasn't sure where to turn. I know he came from a close-knit family, so I asked him if he had shared this struggle with them and requested their help. He explained to me that he had attempted to do that, but while they tried to understand and be supportive, they just didn't know what it was like.

With the words "I thirst" spoken from the cross, Jesus is declaring to each of us in our time of need that he knows what it's like. He has felt pain. He has known suffering.

Are you struggling financially and having a hard time making ends meet? Jesus knows what it's like to be poor. He knows what it's like to be homeless.

Do you feel like you always get the short end and the raw deal? Jesus was born in a manger.

Do you feel like your family doesn't support you? For a while Jesus's own family thought he was crazy.

Has a friend let you down? Jesus was betrayed and abandoned by his closest friends.

Have you been unfairly treated? Jesus faced a series of illegal trials and was unjustly sentenced to death.

Have you experienced anxiety that left you feeling completely overwhelmed? Jesus sweat drops of blood.

Have you experienced physical pain? Jesus had nails driven into his hands and feet.

Jesus knows how you feel.

Hebrews 4:16 points out that because Jesus knows what it's like, we can go to him and find grace in our time of need.

Let us then approach God's throne of grace with confidence, so that we may receive mercy and find grace to help us in our time of need.

Because he knows what it's like, we can approach his throne of grace with confidence and ask for help.

I recently watched a report on a newsmagazine show that exposed some common myths about generosity. People at lower levels of income give around 30 percent more of their income away than those at the upper income levels. They interviewed a lady who regularly gave to help others even though her income wasn't much. She explained why she gave. "I remember a time," she said, "when honestly I couldn't afford lunch money for my son." She knew what it was like, so she wanted to help. Because Jesus knows what it's like, we can approach his throne of grace with confidence and ask for help.

■ ■ ■

A number of years ago I went to Africa on a mission trip and worked among some of the lepers there. It's a horrible disease, and to be honest I tried to minister to them from a distance. I'm not sure I did much good. When I returned home, I was researching some of the ministry work that takes place among lepers and I read about Father Damien. He was a priest who became famous for his willingness to serve lepers. He served at the Kalaupapa Leprosy Settlement on the Hawaiian island of Molokai. For sixteen years he lived in their midst. He learned to speak their language. He bandaged their wounds and embraced the bodies no one else would touch. He organized schools, bands, and choirs. He built homes so the lepers could have shelter. He built two thousand coffins by hand so that, when they died, they could be buried with dignity. He wanted to make this leper village a place to live rather than a place to die.

Father Damien was not careful about keeping his distance. He did nothing to separate himself from the people. He got close. Then one day he stood up and began his sermon with two words: "We lepers . . ." And those two words changed everything. Now he wasn't just there to help them; he was one of them. When Jesus was dying on the cross, he spoke two words that changed everything: "I thirst."

As we approach Easter, I don't know what you are going through or what's been done to you, but you can count on this: Jesus knows. He knows what it's like to be mocked. To be ridiculed. To be abandoned. To be abused. To be beaten. To be betrayed. And knowing that he knows means you don't have to approach the throne of grace and pretend that everything is ok. You can be raw and you can be vulnerable and you can be honest and you can simply say, "I thirst," and he'll understand.

chapter six

Scapegoat

"It is finished."

John 19:30

When Jesus pushed himself upward against the nails in his feet, raised himself upward by the nails through the base of his hands, and exclaimed, "It is finished," it was not a cry of resignation nor an expression of defeat. He did not say, "I am finished." He made a victorious announcement; in fact, the greatest announcement of victory in the history of humanity. The word he shouted from the cross was *"Telestai!"* A general would shout this word in the streets when he returned from the battlefield victorious. He would ride his horse into town, leading his army and his captives, parading the spoils of war for all in the city to see and celebrate.

The word *telestai* also showed up in daily life. When a bill had been paid in full or when a debt had been satisfied, the word would be written across the contract. So, the word had a dual meaning. It was not only a way of declaring victory but also a way to announce completion of payment.

Lifted up on the cross, Jesus fulfilled his messianic mission. He completed his redemptive work on planet Earth. He did for us what we could never do for ourselves. We couldn't make things right with God. We never would have been able to pay the bill for our sin. We could never right our wrongs.

■ ■ ■

A lady in our church recently told me the story about her aunt and uncle. In 1992, on the night before Christmas, they had stepped onto their front porch to turn the Christmas lights out when they noticed a large object wrapped in plastic sitting at the end of their driveway. They unwrapped it and discovered it was a wicker chair that had been stolen from that same front porch eighteen years earlier. There was a note attached to it:

To whom it may concern:

Approximately 13 to 17 years ago my husband stole this wicker rocking chair from the porch of this house. I am ashamed of his behavior and am returning this stolen item. I have since been divorced from my husband and have since been "born again." My life has completely changed and I want to undo any wrongdoing to the best of my ability. I know this chair is not in the same condition as when it was stolen and I apologize. I now live in another state, Tennessee, and am rarely in this vicinity. I realize the cowardly fashion in which I am returning this, but the reason is obvious. I will not bother you again. Please forgive us.

The rocker, along with the letter, was placed in the house where it became a treasured keepsake and the story could be remembered.

Eighteen years later and she was desperate to undo her wrongdoing. The truth is that we all have unfinished business. At some point we all reach the realization that we can't clean up the mess we made. There are too many broken pieces and we can't put them back together. We are desperate to make things right, to get rid of the guilt and shame we feel.

■ ■ ■

Most religious systems give people a way to deal with their guilt and make things right: the Buddhist's eightfold path to enlightenment, the Hindu doctrine of *karma*, the Muslim's code of law that must be followed precisely. In Costa Rica peasants crawl on bloody knees across cobblestone streets as a way to pay penance for their wrongdoing. I recently read about young Lakota warriors who fasten eagle claws to their chest. The claws are then connected to a sacred pole and the warriors fling themselves outward, causing the claws to rip through their skin. Afterward, they enter a sweat lodge until the temperature becomes unbearable—all in an effort to atone for their sins.

We each have our own ways of handling our guilt and shame. See if any of these sound familiar.

1. *Justification.* We deal with our guilt by blaming anything or anyone but ourselves. Many people deal with regret by explaining all the ways it's not their fault and therefore not their responsibility. *If my parents weren't so permissive. If my parents weren't so strict. If my wife wasn't so critical. If my husband wasn't so inattentive. If my boss wasn't so unfair. If the culture wasn't so corrupt.*

2. *Comparison.* We try to make ourselves feel better about our regrets by comparing ourselves to others. I think this is one of the reasons people love gossip magazines and reality TV. Nothing makes me feel like what I've done isn't that big of deal like hearing about what other people have done. It somehow eases my regret when I can say, "Well, at least I didn't . . ."

3. *Distraction.* This is a big one. We know we have unfinished business, but we never stop long enough to look at ourselves in the mirror. We never take the time to reflect upon the decisions we've made. We fill up every inch of our lives with work, relationships, and entertainment. If we ever happen to

have a few spare seconds, we instinctively whip out our cell phones and play games or surf the web.

4. *Escapism.* This is a hard-core form of distraction. A person can't deal with the guilt they feel so they pop a few pills, smoke some weed, get drunk, or pull out the credit card and go on a shopping spree. We self-medicate, trying to treat our guilt and numb the pain of what we have done, if only for a while.

5. *Recompense.* We become aware of the debt we have incurred and desperately try to pay our bill and right our wrongs.

Romans 3:25 says Jesus came and was sacrificed as an atonement for our sins. His blood was the payment. With his death he declared victory over sin. For centuries leading up to this moment, the bill of sin had been deferred.

Leviticus 16 tells us about a day God established for his people called the Day of Atonement. It was a Jewish holy day that was a foreshadowing of what Jesus would one day finish on the cross. Once a year, on the Day of Atonement, the high priest would go out and get two goats. One of the goats was offered as a sacrifice; the blood that was spilled symbolized that without blood there was no forgiveness of sins. Then the priest would take the other goat, place his hands on it, pronounce all of the sins of the people from the previous year, and symbolically put them on that goat. Then he would take it out to the wilderness and let it go to represent that all of those sins were being forgotten. The goat, called the "scapegoat," was symbolically taking them away from the people.

Year after year, generation after generation, the people would do this on the Day of Atonement. It was just part of the sacrificial system God instituted as a way to deal (at least temporarily) with sin. Countless animals were sacrificed, but it was never enough. Then John the Baptist introduced people to Jesus for the first time. John saw Jesus walking toward him, and he pointed to Jesus and said to all the people, "Look, the Lamb of God, who takes away the sin of the world!" (John 1:29). Jesus had come to be our scapegoat. The perfect and final sacrifice. He came to take away the sins of the world. Once and for all, finally and forever, it is finished!

chapter seven

Greater

"Into your hands I commit my spirit."

Luke 23:46

The final words of Jesus from the cross can be traced to the Old Testament; specifically, Psalm 31:5. This is the third time Jesus quoted Scripture from the cross. His suffering was nearly over. He declared victory and knew he was close to being reunited with his Father. Jesus died with the knowledge that the price had been fully paid for the sin of the world. The cup of suffering was empty. And now his mind was clear and engaged as he prayed a quiet and serene prayer to his Father: "Into your hands I commit my spirit."

Luke is the only Gospel writer to record these last words of Jesus. His first words from the cross had been, "Father, forgive them." His last words from the cross were, "Father, into your hands I commit my spirit." "Abba" was Jesus's favorite title for God. It spoke of an intimate relationship from eternity past to this very day between Father, Son, and Holy Spirit.

"Into your hands" speaks of sanctuary. It speaks of safety. It speaks of welcome. It speaks of celebration. It speaks of acceptance. It speaks of love. And these are not ordinary hands. These are the hands that created the universe. These are the hands that molded the earth. These are the hands that formed the physique of humankind. These are our Father's hands.

For nearly fifteen hours Jesus had been in the hands of wicked men. With their hands they beat him, slapped him, abused him, scourged him, and crucified him. But now he returned to his Father's hands.

Jesus died entrusting himself to God. He died submitting to God. And because of the grace that flowed from his cross, we, too, can experience peace in the hour of our transition from this life to the next life. His grace from the cross offers us the only hope that will never disappoint.

■ ■ ■

A few years ago I performed a funeral for a member of our church named Craig Merimee. He had never had any health issues, but after he had spent a few weeks feeling fatigued and having an upset stomach, his wife urged him to visit the doctor. He went the next day and was sent to the ER for testing and a CT scan. Within minutes he was diagnosed with stage IV pancreatic cancer and was given months to live. He and his wife sat in hospital room 313 trying to process what they had just been told. With tears flowing down his cheeks, Craig told his wife that he was deciding right then to trust God no matter what the future held.

I first met Craig four months before the funeral. He and his wife introduced themselves to me after a church service. He asked if I could pray for him because of his recent diagnosis. Craig looked healthy and strong. I immediately felt a connection to him. Besides being about the same age as me, Craig was a father to three beautiful girls, just as I was. I was a little more emotional than I normally would be as I prayed for God's healing.

I checked in with Craig and his wife from time to time in the months ahead. Treatment didn't work. Craig started going downhill fast. His wife was brave but scared. We talked some about how to have conversations with those three little girls about their daddy being sick. What do you say? How do you prepare them?

When I found out about Craig's death, I was not happy with God. I'd seen him work miracles before. Why not this time? And because I could identify with Craig, it felt more personal to me. If God's grace is greater than pancreatic cancer, why didn't God heal him and give him more time with his girls?

As I prepared for the funeral, I went online and read a blog Craig and his wife had started as a way to process what they were going through and communicate with others about it. After a few minutes of reading the first blog entry, I got up and shut my office door so I could cry my way through it. I was so moved by their raw honesty and especially their faith. I eventually came to Craig's final entry. He wrote:

Just looking at myself in the mirror, I can tell my downward spiral has begun. I'm at my all-time low of about 118 pounds. I have an awkward time shaving my face because it is pure bone and I feel like I'm having to shave every bony contour my face has. My yellow eyes constantly remind me my jaundice is settling back in. This pretty much means things are going to eventually start shutting down. There's nothing out there that makes sense for me to do to treat this that we haven't already looked at yet.

I am very motivated about what the future has to offer me. There are a lot of reasons to be excited.

The encouragement I have that my eternal life will be in Heaven and that I will be cancer free soon puts a smile on my face.[*]

I finally arrived at the very last sentence. It was just three words followed by five exclamation points. Craig's final words:

God is good!!!!!

[*] Craig Merimee, "My End of the Road," *The Merimee's Journey*, February 29, 2012, http://merimeejourney.blogspot.com/2012/02/my-end-of-road.html.

The reason Craig could make those the final words of his blog post is because of the final words of Jesus from the cross. Because of grace, the same peace Jesus had with his final breath is the peace we can have in our final moments.

■ ■ ■

Jesus's death on the cross caused the earth to shake, rocks to split, and the sky to go dark. His death on the cross caused the temple veil, as thick as the breadth of a man's hand, to be split from top to bottom like tissue paper, as though ripped by giant, invisible shears. Jesus lives evermore. His presence cannot be confined to a tomb or imprisoned by death. Jesus is Lord of life. He is Lord over death. He is the resurrection and the life.

And because Jesus died and rose again, we can know that grace is always greater. No matter what. No matter what you've done. No matter what's been done to you. No matter what you're going through—grace is still greater. Grace may not heal your husband but it will hold you up. Grace may not cure your cancer but it will carry you through. Grace may not rescue you from your circumstances but it will redeem your circumstances.

Grace is greater than the diagnosis you were given, the abuse you experienced, the secrets you've kept, the addiction you've battled. Grace is greater than anything you go through and anything you have done.

No matter how far you've fallen. No matter how often you've failed. Grace is still greater. No matter how many times you've relapsed, or how often your resolve has collapsed. Grace is still greater.

You say to yourself, *Not after what I did. Some things can't be undone. I crossed the line. There's no going back.* But grace is greater than what you did, because it's based on what Jesus has done.

You may have dropped out or been kicked out. You may have been knocked down or locked up. You may have cheated or been cheated on. But what's most important about you is that, no matter what, the greatness of God's grace is true and by his grace he can make all things new.

Grace is powerful enough to erase your guilt. Grace is big enough to cover your shame.

Grace is real enough to heal your relationships.

Grace is strong enough to hold you up when you are weak.

Grace is sweet enough to cure your bitterness.

Grace is satisfying enough to deal with your disappointment.

Grace is beautiful enough to redeem your brokenness.

You may have given up on grace, but grace hasn't given up on you. It's no accident that you are reading this. It's God's grace at work right now. His grace has chased you down and his grace will help you up. Because no matter what you've done, no matter what's been done to you, no matter what you're going through—grace is *still* greater.

▓ ▓ ▓

So, where are you in all this?

If you're a Christian, my guess is you struggle with accepting God's grace in at least one area. Let me make one suggestion: talk to somebody. Talk to a good friend or a spiritual mentor. Let them know how and why you're struggling. God never meant for us to do life on our own, and sometimes a single conversation can make a big difference.

If you're not a Christian, I want to encourage you take a step of faith—to accept God's grace for your sins and begin your grace-filled journey with Jesus. I also encourage you to talk to somebody. Maybe you could find a Bible-believing church in your area and schedule an appointment with a pastor. If you received this book as a gift, maybe you could talk with whoever gave it to you. Tell them you want to begin (or renew) your journey of faith, and you're wondering if they can help you so you don't have to do it by yourself.

Remember: whatever it is that holds us back, grace is greater. May we receive God's grace in our lives, and may we give to others what was first given to us.

Kyle Idleman is teaching pastor at Southeast Christian Church in Louisville, Kentucky, the fifth largest church in America, where he speaks to more than twenty thousand people each weekend. He is the bestselling and award-winning author of *Not a Fan* as well as *Grace Is Greater*, *Gods at War*, and *The End of Me*. He is a frequent speaker for national conventions and in influential churches across the country. Kyle and his wife, DesiRae, have four children and live on a farm in Kentucky, where he doesn't do any actual farming.

CONNECT
WITH **KYLE**!

KyleIdleman

🐦 KyleIdleman

KyleIdleman.com

Shop a library of resources from City on a Hill featuring

KYLE IDLEMAN

cityonahillstudio.com

 SERIES   JOURNAL   LEADER'S GUIDE  SMALL GROUP   PASTOR'S KIT

MADE ALIVE

— IN CHRIST —

GraceIsGreaterStudy.com

20% OFF YOUR PURCHASE
Use Coupon Code MGBK20